Poems for Living

Sept. 11, 1993

Happy Birthday Eleanor -
I hope the beautiful Poems
in this book bring you much
Love, joy & Comfort -
    They are So Meaningful - Profound
& Deep - they touched my Heart & I
hope they touch yours the Same Way -
Ruth Clingerman is a Sister in the
Spirit - for Our Spirits Touched - May
She reach Out thru the Pages
Capturing your Heart, Touching your
Spirit & filling you With Much
Love - Peace & Joy - My birthday
Wish for you - Now & Always
            Love   Dawn

Poems for Living

Ruth Malan Clingerman

VANTAGE PRESS
New York

FIRST EDITION

Copyright © 1991 by Ruth Malan Clingerman

Published by Vantage Press, Inc.
516 West 34th Street, New York, New York 10001

Manufactured in the United States of America
ISBN: 0-533-09405-4

Library of Congress Catalog Card No.: 90-91456

0 9 8 7 6 5 4 3 2 1

To the memory of my
former English teacher, Esther Hager

Contents

Foreword

Ruth Malan was born on September 1, 1927, the third of six children of a Missouri farm couple. Her parents were largely uneducated, but they provided a good home by means of love, decency, and hard work.

Ruth grew up in circumstances that would make most people quail—her family was impoverished, with no electricity or indoor plumbing. However, Ruth did have one very important asset—a vital, yearning intellect. She made the most of her education in a one-room schoolhouse, and later at high school in Linn, Missouri, with then a population of 500. Early in her life, she developed a passion for the English language—especially for the expressive power of words well-crafted into poetry. She read the great poets, and took pen to paper herself with a dream of someday, perhaps, making her own contribution to this great body.

Other dreams abounded as well. Upon her graduation as valedictorian of her high school class, Ruth felt the need to achieve more than what her rural life offered. She bravely set off for the "big city" of Washington, D.C., to seek her fortune. Her ability with words served her well as a secretary, and eventually she worked her way to the position of administrative aide to the Assistant Secretary of Defense.

There was yet another dream—on June 11, 1949, she married a handsome sailor, fresh from the "Big War," by the name of Joe Clingerman.

Over the next quarter of a century, Ruth's dreams were mingled, the happy with the sad. She reared three sons and lost another son and a daughter in infancy. She sacrificed some of her most deep-seated dreams out of her abiding love and support of her husband's railroad career and for her children's welfare. Yet, through all of the many personal upheavals of moving the family, starting a career anew, making ends meet, confronting life, confronting death—the poetic muse kept persisting. By now the dream was irresistible; it had grown inexorably powerful upon the nourishment of life experience.

Although Ruth has pursued a career for many years, she now has taken pause from the canvas of her life to publish this collection of her work thus far. Her poems abound with energy and with imagery; yet her work does not require the aid of a dictionary to understand or to appreciate. The reader will most readily identify with her subject matter—and with her compassion and her search for meaning. She expresses the fear of dying and the fear of living; the joy of living and the joy of dying—thus she captures the essence of human uncertainty and ambivalence. Her work epitomizes the need of human transcendence: She will clean the house, tend the garden, play with the cat—then she will soar beyond the mountain peaks and clouds right to the very throne of Almighty God. She is patently qualified to do all of this.

Ruth's dream has now become the accomplishment of reality. Regardless of posterity's assessment of this volume, Mom is a remarkable woman of whom I am justly proud. And her dream lives on—a bit of it in all of us.

Philip Clingerman
Somerset, New Jersey

Preface

The proudest accomplishment of my lifetime will always be the three wonderful and worthwhile sons whom I have presented to the world. They are my crowning joy, and nothing I can ever do will exceed this achievement.

There came a time, however, when I felt the need to leave something more of myself to posterity. With the thought of its coming to fruition but a dream, I plodded along with my verses for my own enjoyment, as well as that of my family and my friends.

My first poem (a sonnet—"Shakespeare") was composed in senior English as a class assignment of my teacher, Esther Hager, to whose memory this book is dedicated. It was under her caring tutelage that I developed my knowledge of and love for poetry.

During my late teens and early twenties, several poems were written and added to my collection. After my marriage and the ensuing child-rearing years, my inspiration was repressed by domestic burdens and economic hardship, and the muse lay dormant.

During the succeeding years, several verses were produced; but it was not until I shared a sampling of my poems with my former grammar school teacher, Grace Bacon Ferrier (herself an author), that I was encouraged to look toward publication. "Miss Grace" vehemently and convincingly assured me that I had something to say that would be appreciated by the reading public.

In Mrs. Hager's literature class, we were encouraged to analyze the possible motives and emotions of the author to see how he was affected by life experience and, in common parlance, where he was coming from. If you choose to use that approach with this volume, I do not object. But it would please me, as well, if you would apply any message to your own life in hope that it might enlarge your perceptions in a constructive way.

While compiling this work, I attempted to study a "poet's handbook," and I found many areas of disagreement with the author. He believes the poet should never preach to the reader; I have at least exhorted. He wrote that poems should not be titled for qualities; I have "Courage" and "Resolve" at least. He further wrote that form was more important than the message; my poems are largely messages enhanced by pleasant meter and rhyme. Considering that I may be doing many things contrary to accepted practice produced the tongue-in-cheek poem, "Ragged Underwear."

While browsing in a bookstore, I came across an inch-thick volume entitled *How to Read and Understand Poetry*. I deplore the necessity for such a volume; and, if my verses are not understandable at the first reading, I apologize to the reader.

While I would appreciate critical acclaim and the approbation of fellow poets, my chief reward would be to reach average people and share with them the heights and depths of my life experiences. I feel that I speak to them and hope I have reproduced some of the joys, fears, anxieties, hopes, faith, and humor that are so much a part of our daily lives.

So, come laugh with me, love with me, cry with me; fear with me, pray with me, sigh with me as you peruse the contents of this little book.

Start at the beginning, the end, or the middle; pick it

up and put it down; read and re-read it; and, when you have finished, share it with a friend!

—Ruth Malan Clingerman

Acknowledgments

My sincere thanks to

my friends and family
who offered their encouragement

my friend, Lorraine Carchidi,
who was my "first reader"

my son Philip
for assistance with editing and arranging

my husband
who helped me find a publisher

and my former teacher
Grace Bacon Ferrier
who gave me the final push

Springtime

A fresh, new softness fills the fragrant air
As springtime ventures slowly forth again,
Dispersing winter's bleak and bitter fare
And bringing hope and promise through the land.

The tender grass that lies beneath our feet,
All patterned in the maple's dappled shade,
While growing lush and green with dew replete,
Has yet to know the biting mower's blade.

The myriad birds send forth their clarion notes—
A warning of approach to their domains—
A symphony of trilling from their throats—
An artless Babel in their sweet refrains.

Now patter, patter falls the gentle rain,
Rejuvenating winter-weary Earth,
While tapping, tapping on our window pane
And bringing every leaf and bud to birth.

The fragrance of the blossoms fills the air;
Their soft and breathless beauty now unfolds—
A Nature's wonderland where all was bare—
The blue, the white, the pink, the red, the gold.

So swiftly flies each precious, balmy day
To draw this happy season to a close
That June comes tripping lightly after May
And brings the bloom of summer and the rose.

Yet when this special glory long has passed,
Its treasured mem'ries to my mind will bring
The sweet remembrance which shall ever last—
And give unto my heart eternal spring.

While in the Bleakest Hours

While in the bleakest hours I wait alone,
My dark thoughts conjure up an image grave
And terror grips the marrow of my bone,
And apprehension does my thoughts enslave.
I cannot venture that tomorrow's dawn
Will find all's well and all my fears allay.
I struggle for the strength to carry on
To find a brightness in another day.
But night envelops my eroding fears;
I cannot prophesy the dawn's release.
Besieging Heaven's portals with my tears,
I pray with hopeless heart for promised peace.
Awaiting respite with a tortured breath,
A thousand times I die my coward's death.

My Children

I bore them in my womb with love
And nurtured them with tender care;
I watched them grow in form and mind
And tried each hope and fear to share.

I set their feet on proper paths
And carefully prepared their way;
Then, finally, the cord was cut—
And now I stand and watch and pray.

Just Open Your Door

Just open up your door a little wider
So I can know what dwells inside your heart;
Then I'll not be a casual outsider
If you will only let the portals part.

I'll learn what brings you joy or causes sorrow;
Your smallest wish will be my fervent goal;
I'll learn your hopes and wishes for tomorrow,
As bells of happiness their message toll.

I'll know which dreams to loose and which to tether,
And we'll be blest with love forevermore;
Our separate hearts will beat as one together
If you will only open wide the door.

4

Challenge

Dare to be brave!
You who would tremble in face of disaster,
Think not too strongly of consequence grave;
Safety you seek will arrive much the faster.
Dare to be brave!

Dare to be brave!
Act in a trice without thought of revision;
Think of the care and the worry you save.
You who would falter in time of decision,
Dare to be brave!

Dare to be brave!
What if you o'erleap the bonds of convention,
Which at the best our advancement enslave?
Learn that the act ever proves the intention.
Dare to be brave!

Dare to be brave!
Freedom from fear is a glorious treasure;
Never to cringing or doubt be a slave.
Life will hold vigor and glory and pleasure
If you are brave!

Passage

One day I'll spread my dormant wings and rise
To flee the tumult of this earthly place,
And pass in final triumph through the skies
To meet our blest Redeemer face to face.

Relinquishing my tattered human gown
To be forever robed in gossamer,
There I will lay my vain transgressions down,
Beyond all mortal tendency to err.

Abandoning invalid covenants,
Surrendering all doctrines that are trite,
I'll find a tenet that this glory grants,
Beyond Earth's power, beyond all human might.

For there I'll step upon another shore,
No more a stranger on a foreign strand,
But sheltered safe from care forevermore—
A pilgrim home within the Promised Land.

Bereavement

"My sympathy," my dear friend said,
While holding tight my hand;
And since my father lay in death,
She did not understand
How I could face this somber day
With minor show of loss;
She did not know what went before—
How painful was the cost,
When years ago, his fading eyes
Had gazed at me, and then
He shook his head as if to say
He did not understand.
My heart was dealt a cruel blow,
As sad as death, for when
He did not recognize my face,
I lost my father then.

Christy

Christy is my little one;
Christy is my pretty one;
Christy is my moon and sun—
I love my little Christy.

Christy's hair is golden-hued;
Christy's eyes are golden, too;
Christy's love is ever true—
I love my little Christy.

Christy's hair is soft and long;
Christy's pearly teeth are strong;
Christy hums a little song—
I love my little Christy.

Christy's touch is very dear;
Christy nestles without fear;
I shout for all the world to hear—
I love my pretty kitty!

Should I Be Doomed

Should I be doomed to spend my life in grief
And slowly sip the bitter cup of woe
Till into dark Gethsemane I go
In neither Heav'n nor earth to find relief;
If I must forfeit all my dreams of fame
And live, instead, in hopeless, black despair
With anguish, tumult, loneliness, and care
My lone possessions—all my earthly claim,
Then may some downcast soul be filled with glee;
May it have strength—enabled be to dare;
And may some other heart be light and free
To live its happy, unimpeded way
By reason of the burdens that I bear.

Miles to Go

Time was when sunlight kissed her hair
    And glistened off its auburn hue—
Her step was light; her hands were sure;
    Her hopes were high and dreams were new.

Though now her form is stooped and frail,
    And though her hair has turned to snow,
She still has many dreams to dream
    And vows to keep and miles to go.

Farmer's Prayer

Just a few more days till Sunday
For the tillin' of the sod;
Then the preacher will be preachin'
And a-tellin' us of God.

Dear Lord, grant me strength 'n' vigor
As I work from sun to sun;
I've so many jobs awaitin'
And so many chores undone.

I'm up before the rooster's crowin',
And I work the livelong day
In the mowin' of the pasture
And the pitchin' of the hay.

I must keep my body movin'
For all my weariness allows—
There's the groomin' of the horses
And the milkin' of the cows.

There's the feedin' of the chickens
And the gatherin' of the eggs,
Pausin' for a cup of coffee
And a-savorin' of the dregs.

There's the settin' of the fenceposts
And the sloppin' of the hogs;
There's the cuttin' down of timber
And the sawin' up the logs.

There's the hoein' of the garden
And a-harvestin' the crops
And the pickin' the wild berries
Till I feel that I will drop.

Just a few more days till Sunday—
When you're workin' with the sod,
You have faith and understandin',
And you learn a lot of God.

What Did We Know?

The knowledge of the fading centuries
Sits idly on the narrow, dusty shelves
While we, unmindful of the penalties,
Proceed to please and gratify ourselves.

Each generation struggles yet again
And surely must experience once more
The errors that were once our father's bane—
Harsh lessons that we casually ignore.

As like a vacant student we decline
To profit from our tortured history,
The teachings of the years are left behind
In shallow thrashings or in reverie.

And when the final epitaph is graved,
What will the damning, slurring record show,
While we assess the energies we gave—
What did we know; what did we really know?

To Christopher

Free spirit on a Harley bike,
You speed o'er hill and dale and plain;
Not wet of rain nor dark of night
Can e'er your blithesome flight restrain.

And few can know the vibrant joy
That carries you along Life's way—
My happy, unencumbered boy
Who turns my hair to shades of gray.

Yet in my bosom, pride I find—
And you're with such endearment blest,
Despite the cares that weight my mind,
I could not ever love you less.

On Racial Prejudice

Far be my heart from pride and hate;
　Far be my soul from spite;
When through mere accident of birth,
　My skin is colored white.

13

To a Worm

You are quite lowly, Worm,
Crawling from door to door—
You creature of ignoble caste,
Most degrading metaphor.

Senseless to unfeeling shoes
Crushing your life's breath,
Leaving you but a sticky spot
With none to mourn your death.

You shun the beaks of hungry birds
Out in the woods so wild
And roll in suffocating agony
In the glass jar of a child.

We pierce you with a jagged hook
And dangle you from a line,
And fishes at your vitals chew
While we on the bank recline.

We torment you incessantly
And laugh to see you squirm;
Why not, offensive creature?
You're just a hideous worm!

Despicable emblem of inferiority!
Detestable vermin of the sod!
Slimy, fuzzy, revolting—
Insignificant creation of God!

Yet you clamor not for high renown,
For power, fame, or pelf—
Oh, for your grace and character
To be your honest self!

The Downhill Side

When you've reached Life's mountain summit
And are on the downhill side,
You expect an easy journey, I should think;
But be careful of the avalanche—
Be wary of the slide;
Remember every chasm has its brink.

"Downhill" takes a somber meaning
As your aches and pains attest;
And silver hairs appear among the gold;
You can feel the muscles weaken,
And your functioning grow less,
And you're startled by the knowledge you are old.

After years of strife and labor,
You expect a sweet surcease,
And you yearn for pleasure of a broader scope;
But regard your stars as lucky
If your greatest prize is peace,
And you settle for a portion of your hope.

Keep a cheerful heart within you,
And you'll triumph in the end,
For it's joy that makes our weary world go 'round;
Take delight in all your neighbors,
While you cherish friend and kin,
And accept whatever destiny you've found.

Dent de Lion

They dot the early April lawn
Lake nature's coins of purest gold,
And lift their faces to the sun,
Ignoring spring's residual cold.

They're picked by tiny toddler hands—
Their friendly stems without a thorn—
To make a quaint, homespun bouquet
To offer on a dewy morn.

Some will mature with fleecy heads,
Gray guardians of the crisp, spring day,
Until they're wafted by a breeze
And lightly spirited away.

They will endure the mower's blade
And bask in summer's heat and rain,
Then hide until another spring
To show a sunny face again.

To a Cigarette

Just a simple, white stick of purported
    sensual pleasure,
You bring agonizing destruction to thousands
    of partakers
Who don't, or care not to, recognize
    your villainy.

You lie in feigned innocence on a
    crystal saucer,
While your acrid emissions swirl in
    cloudy fantasies,
Polluting the space of those in your
    proximity.

The innocent, too, must breathe your
    smoky venom;
Young and old alike, with no choice of
    indulgence,
Are callously exposed to your virulent
    vapors.

Oh, lethal white instrument of human
    destruction,
How many needless and tragic deaths must
    we number
Before you are rejected and sent into
    oblivion?

For each of us there will be day of
    final reckoning,
When Fate will decree who stays and who's
    to go;
And choice will no longer be an open course
    of action.

I Drank the Beauty

I drank the beauty of this earthly sphere,
Reflecting not indifferent hand of chance;
But when I would proclaim for all to hear,
I grieved because my soul lacked utterance.
There as I wrestled with my stubborn pen,
I breathed to Heav'n a deep, sincere request;
Then through my writhing soul's wild, surging din,
A sweet, unearthly voice thus me addressed:

"Do not my marvels into words transmute,
But put thy aching heart and mind at rest.
Fret not, my child, because thy tongue is mute;
These wonders are by silence best expressed."
I paused, and felt a flood of sweet release
That filled my soul with all-abiding peace.

Indifference

Our love has lost its meaning;
 Our rainbow's turned to dust;
There is no caring in you;
 There is no truth or trust.

Your words have cut like razors;
 Your smile has lost its beam;
Your arms no longer hold me;
 You've scuttled all my dreams.

My life will be made over
 To fit another plan;
I'll find another rainbow,
 And take a different stand.

It doesn't really matter—
 The things you do or say;
My heart is just a muscle
 For pumping blood all day.

Valley Winter

The hoary wind blasted down
  the shivering valley,
Bringing chilling shrouds
  of snow and sleet;
Black smoke from
  the isolated chimneys
Streamed as from
  a fleeing locomotive.

Aspens quivered their
  fairy dance;
Macho oaks sparsely shed
  their masculinity;
Maples cascaded
  in crimson and gold;
Pines and spruces remained
  the forest sentinels.

A small animal peeked furtively
  from its hidden lair
And disappeared
  into the comforting confines;
Night settled in
  to bring a colder cold,
And bleak winter came
  to the valley.

To Philip
(*On His 20th Birthday*)

Two swift decades have slipped away—
  Today you stand a man—
Tomorrow's promise in your eyes;
  Your future in your hands.

The tumult of the teens is past;
  You've won a battle star;
But Challenge still awaits without
  And taunts you where you are.

Behind you stands a host of friends,
  And those who love you best,
Whose faith will never flag nor fail
  As Life your fiber tests.

And so upon your future days,
  May fortune always shine,
And God our Father bless and keep
  This splendid son of mine.

Scott

I do not know Thy ways, dear God;
  I cannot understand—
What justice lies in man's domain;
  What works are by Thy hand?

Did you his virtues fairly weigh?
  Did you assess my cost?
Why did his life's breath ebb away
  And leave me with my loss?

Forgive my vascillating faith,
  My anger, my distress;
Assuage my overwhelming grief;
  Remove my bitterness.

Was this Your answer to my prayers,
  Or was it hand of Fate?
God, grant that understanding comes
  And patience while I wait.

The Walk-On

The human has a pair of legs
On which are two appendages
In common parlance known as feet—
Sometimes foul and sometimes sweet—
These feet are prone to many woes—
Bunions, corns, and hammertoes,
Forgetting not the fearful spur
That can upon the heel occur.
The dreaded itch of athletes
Is sometimes foisted on the feet,
While calluses and warts assail
To make the average person quail.

If human feet did not abound,
We'd have much trouble getting 'round
To move ourselves from here to there;
We'd hardly make it anywhere.

A message in these humble lines
Is what I'm hoping you will find—
So whether foul or whether sweet,
Be kind to your poor, faithful feet.

November Roses

Outside my frosty window I behold
My faded, wintry garden, bleak and sere;
The rose has lost its scarlet and its gold,
And snow foretells the dying of the year.

Sweet summer's glow of beauty now is past—
Like summer's dreams and fantasies, is flown;
Yet on the still-green leaves my faith is cast;
Like tender seeds, my future hopes are sown.

The melancholy haunt of summer's bier
Shall not impose upon me gloom nor woe,
For in my heart I keep my fancies dear—
Like autumn roses bowing in the snow.

Mary Carol

'Twas on the eve of Christmas
  She chose to come to birth—
A season of rejoicing—
  A time for song and mirth.

We named her for the mother
  Of the holy Christmas Child,
And for the season's music
  So joyous and so mild.

She was too small and fragile
  For human hands to hold;
She never knew a mother's touch
  Or felt my arms enfold.

Four days we had a daughter
  And didn't dare to dream;
Our prayers were ineffectual
  In Fate's eternal scheme.

They buried her in winter
  In a cold December rain,
While I stood at my window
  With bosom numb with pain.

If I could find a reason
  This sorrow had to be,
My heart might find some meaning
  And rest more tranquilly.

That fine old word, "acceptance,"
  Is the rock to which I'll hold
And pray that time will soften
  And the memory grow old.

What Do You Do with a Broken Toe?

So what do you do with a broken toe?
First, you grit your teeth so the pain won't show;
Then you tape it tight to a brother toe,
And off you go—ho, ho, ho, ho!

You walk on your heel with a gait so slow,
And you hope in your heart that the pain won't grow;
Hippity, hoppity—along you go;
And that's what you do with a broken toe!

To My Husband

You came to me in Life's still morning dew
And placed the kiss of promise on my eyes;
You stirred a love so deep and brightly new
And spurred my faltering heart to recognize
The joy of giving; and as one we trod
Life's steep and ofttimes rough and rocky road,
We found a special fellowship with God
That filled our lives and lightened every load.
We learned the agony of death and grief;
We shared with joy each little happiness
And grew in strength and love beyond belief;
And I, who with such fortune richly blest,
Shall with a grateful heart still fast adore
And stay beside you, Love, forevermore.

Counting My Blessings

Each morning when I lift my eyes,
My blessings shower over me;
I view the sun, the clouds, the skies
And thank my God that I can see.

I set my feet on daily tours,
A bit rebuffed if they should balk;
But though they're tired and slow and sore,
I thank my God that I can walk.

My voice no longer soars in song—
My vocal powers are strained and weak;
But, oh, the pleasure I have known;
So thank you, God, that I can speak.

My ears can catch the poignant calls
Of joy and love and hope and fear;
I may not mark the sparrow's fall,
But thank you, God, that I can hear.

My mind with images is lade,
With thoughts that weave and interlink;
And though my memory may fade,
I thank you, God, that I can think.

Though wealth is sparse and fame is coy
And high acclaim may not abound,
My still-glad heart near bursts with joy
Because of blessings I have found.

The Dripping of the Water

The careless word, the gruff retort,
The thoughtless and abrupt reply
Can etch like acid in the soul
Where soft and tender feelings lie;
The statement better left unsaid
Can sear the senses finely-blown;
  And the dripping of the water
  Surely wears away the stone.

The dream that's crushed while yet unborn
Can never hope to raise its head;
The callous taunt, the cruel jest
Will foster hopelessness instead;
While under subjugation's yoke,
There cannot be a dream full-blown;
  And the dripping of the water
  Surely wears away the stone.

Indifference lifts its silent shield
And o'er the hurt a callus grows;
Sore feelings shrink within a shell,
Their wounds no longer to expose;
And joy has long since ceased to be,
No longer to reclaim its own;
  And the dripping of the water
  Surely wears away the stone.

To Michael

A doctor of philosophy!
What high regard you now command!
Doors open wide for your degree;
You hold tomorrow in your hand!

On subjects all you have a view;
Your erudition knows no bound;
Your reasoning is ever true;
Your logic sharp and ever sound.

Colossal was the price you paid
Through years of struggle—sleepless nights;
With courage dauntless, unafraid,
You rose triumphant from the fight.

But somehow in these learning years
Your childhood faith seemed cast aside;
And in my heart are secret fears
For whether faith does yet abide.

Now with your formal studies o'er,
It's time to calculate the cost
And tally up the final score
Of what you gained and what you lost.

On My Birthday

I see the morn dawn clear and bright
   On this, my natal day;
The gay lark's song dispels the night
   And brings the sun's soft ray.

But should the sun refuse to shine
   And clouds decline to part,
I still can feel a warming glow
   In reaches of my heart.

The greetings of both friend and kin
   Sound in a friendly way
To make my spirits lift with joy
   On this, my special day.

I number yet another year
   And hope I'm wiser still—
Another year to love and learn,
   With service to fulfill.

I shall not count the tiny flames
   That on my cake appear;
But count, instead, with thankful heart,
   The blessings of the year.

What greater cause to celebrate,
   Rejoicing on my way—
God gave me chance of lasting life
   On this, my natal day.

There Breathes a Man

There breathes a man who walks without a fear,
Who feels his strength throughout his mortal frame,
Who visualizes life without a peer,
Whose goals lead only onward unto fame.

While flaunting pride before all human eyes,
He scales his mountains, sails his boundless seas,
But with each passing day his future lies
A simple heartbeat from eternity.

He boldly stalks and struts his arrogance,
And does not recognize his finite state;
He leaves Hereafter to the hand of chance,
Implying immortality can wait.

He, too, shall count each faint and fragile breath,
And thereupon shall know the taste of death.

On Housecleaning

It's Saturday, and cleaning time;
   So, somehow, if I must,
I'll put my house in proper form
   And rearrange the dust.

I'll sweep the rug and wax the floor;
   I'll wash the clothes, I trust;
But mostly in this ritual,
   I'll rearrange the dust.

Although my house is neat and clean
   Because I've worked and fussed,
I'll tell the world I'm plenty bored
   With rearranging dust.

My aspirations fly quite high—
   This role I must adjust—
For I am anchored down to earth
   By rearranging dust.

Laments of the Viet Nam War
(Song Cycle)

I. Lament on Leaving

Oh, must I go when life looms large before me?
When hearts are young and love is all aglow?
What holy cause has stunned my life so sorely,
And left me with a sadness few may know?

When time hangs long, I'll think of my tomorrows
And of the dreams I'd always hoped would be;
I'll say a prayer to help me through my sorrows,
And keep my courage high, my spirit free.

Goodbye, my friends, I'm sorry now to leave you;
Goodbye, my love, please keep your sacred vow;
If only through the grace of God, believe me,
I'll come back home again to you somehow.

Refrain:

Oh, when will I see home again?
When is my journey o'er?
When will I hold my love again
With peace forevermore?

II. Letter of Lament

Dear Mom, I'm tired—so very tired;
  This jungle's hot and deep,
But we must take Hill Twenty-One
  Before we stop to sleep.

I'm tired of death; I'm tired of war;
  I'm tired of blood and pain;
But peacetime seems so very far
  Till I see home again.

So send all prayers that you can give
  To ease my aching heart;
Hard roads I tread; long nights I live
  Till nevermore we part.

Refrain:
  For we must do what we must do,
  And with God's help,
  We'll see it through.
  It's hard to sip the bitter dew,
  But we must do what we must do.

III. Lament of the Abandoned Husband

Our love was like a full-blown rose of summer;
I never thought I'd see it fall apart;
But now its shattered petals lie forsaken
Like shadows on my lonely, aching heart.

The time that tried your love was unrelenting—
As long for you as it was long for me;
But with the promise of our love before me,
I lived for joy that never was to be.

I curse the war that tore our lives asunder;
I dread anew the dawning of each day.
In saving face for Sam's colossal blunder,
Our land decreed the innocent must pay.

Good-bye, my love, we'll never see tomorrow
Or hand-in-hand watch all our dreams come true;
May you know happiness in fullest measure
And may time heal the hurt I feel for you.

IV. Lament of the Disabled Veteran

My country called, and I said goodbye,
But never knew all the reasons why;
And I don't know now when it's far too late
Except to ponder a soldier's fate.
And it's hard to feel like you say I should
As I walk the streets on my legs of wood.

My hands are skilled, and my mind is strong;
But the jobs are few and the talent wrong;
So I hang my head and I take your dole,
Though it tastes like gall to my bitter soul.
And it's hard to feel like you say I should
As I walk the streets on my legs of wood.

My love was true but I let her go;
And I felt the pain only few may know;
She must love again, and I know she can—
Won't keep her tied to only half a man.
And it's hard to feel like you say I should
As I walk the streets on my legs of wood.

V. Bereaved Father's Lament

With tousled curls and sparkling eyes
And chubby little legs that run,
Your mother sang you lullabies;
  But they let you die,
  My son, my son!

Your baseball glove and hockey skates,
The thrill of your young life begun,
Your books and school and movie dates;
  But they let you die,
  My son, my son!

Too many guns, too many fights,
Too many victories to be won,
Too many endless days and nights;
  And they let you die,
  My son, my son!

Where are my hopes; where are my dreams?
Now only tears like rivers run,
While moonlight on my sorrow beams—
  For they let you die,
  My son, my son!

Ragged Underwear
(On Reading a High-Flown Poetry "Handbook")

I do not know a stanza from a strope;
I do not know, nor do I really care;
But this I care, and this I truly hope—
That I can write in ragged underwear.

High education has not been my forte;
My skills, if any, are not finely honed;
But try I will to all my powers exhort
To extricate the meter's flesh from bone.

My love of words continues through the years;
My soul cries out in faith and love and care,
That I may bring you happiness and tears
And learn to write in ragged underwear.

Long may the mighty odes and epics roll;
A sharp salute to all the fancy fare;
Just let me satisfy my heart and soul,
And ply my pen in ragged underwear.

So, though my skills be many, few, or none,
I'll trust I have a worthy thought to share,
And in my numbered days beneath the sun,
Pursue the muse in ragged underwear.

The Rose beside the Gate

The pure white rose beside the gate
Grew lush with green canes overrun,
And waves of lovely blossoms pale
Cascaded in the bright June sun.

A pretty child with winsome ways
Inhaled its heady fragrance rare,
And on her confirmation day,
Wore pure white roses in her hair.

As days flew by, the child grew tall,
And on her happy wedding day—
So fair of form, so full of grace—
Bore pure white blooms in her bouquet.

Relentless Time, one hapless day,
Laid claim unto her spirit brave;
And they who laid her form to rest
Placed pure white blossoms on her grave.

The rose still blooms when it is June,
Indifferent to human fate,
Dispensing still its sweet perfume—
The pure white rose beside the gate.

Auntie Jude

The children sit about her knee
　To hear of olden days,
Their faces bright with eagerness
　For tales of former ways.

Her many books are highly stacked
　To ceiling from the floor;
The children hang on every word
　And always beg for more.

The magic of her music flows
　From skillful fingertips;
The beauty of her voice spills forth
　From practiced, flawless lips.

Her gracious touch is felt by all—
　So tender and so kind—
And many vistas she reveals,
　Despite the fact she's blind.

Hero Worship

I worshipped once an earthly man
With all the ardor of my soul
Until I, conscience-stricken, paused
To wonder what the Lord of Old
Who ruled, "Before me have no God,"
When looking on my sin, would say.

But that Omniscient Mind
Knew that ere long I'd find
No mortal is divine
And idols' feet are clay.

Tomorrow

When the darkness fades to silver,
We will greet another dawn
With another prize to capture
And another race to run.

Will we welcome it with gladness;
Will our special dreams unfold;
Will our spirits meet the challenge;
Will our hearts be brave and bold?

Will our hands accept the labor
That unto our lot may fall;
Will our voices rise in triumph
As we heed tomorrow's call?

Will our feet be fleet and willing
To accept the journey's toll;
Will we greet the day with valor
And with richness of the soul?

With the joy of Life within us,
Let's not tarry on our way
And rejoice in each tomorrow,
For we've learned to love today!

The Red Birds

"Remember me at Christmastime,"
My mother said to me,
"For when you place these bright red birds
Upon your Christmas tree,
I'll come to you in loving thoughts,
Wherever I may be."

Now many Christmases have gone
Since Mother ceased to be
And went to seek her final home
To rest eternally;
Yet she is ever in my heart
As I deck out the tree.

Though years may come and years may go,
She lives in memory—
The loving hand, the kindly voice
All seem so real to me
Each time I place the bright red birds
Upon the Christmas tree.

The Woman

Her face was creased by instruments of time;
Her hair was tinted silver by the years;
And on her face a written record stood
Of heartaches, passions, happiness, and tears.

All those she met were prone to stop and speak;
Their greetings she returned with smiles and sighs;
Yet with her fading eyesight, dim and weak,
She read with pain the pity in their eyes.

Did they not know that in her youthful prime
The beauties of this day she far surpassed?
Did they not know that proud, wild heart beat still,
Although the fleeting beauty did not last?

She gazed upon her wrinkled, trembling hand;
She shook her scraggy locks no longer gold
And grieved because they did not understand,
But looked on her with pity—called her old.

Raised Ranch

I look out my window
  Into a trunk
Halfway up a tree;
I must peer down
  To see the ground,
And this distresses me.

Of all the things
  I've left behind,
I'll miss forevermore
  My lovely picture window
On the ground level floor.

To My Friend Mary
(*On Another Relocation*)

Oh, can you share my cross for but a day?
And would you blot the cheek where tears have flowed?
I know, my friend, you'd try to find a way
To smooth a path along my rocky road.

You see, my friend, you've walked this path before;
You've felt the anguish of a soul near gone;
You've known the doubt that steals inside the door
And found the strength you need to carry on.

You've felt the wrench that tore away your home,
That took good friends and left you sad, forlorn;
You've had to learn to brave new worlds alone
And stand in tears amid the alien corn.

And so you know my load I bear alone,
No matter what the pain, the strain, the cost;
Until the glimmer of dawn's light has shown,
The night is mine—the tears, the fears, the cross.

Tomorrow's Promise

As we trudge along Life's highway
And are greeted with rebuffs,
While misfortune and remorse both take their tolls,
We must lift our drooping spirits,
Though the journey may be rough,
And assure that trials never scar our souls.

While our sorrows may be heavy,
Still in Fate's eternal scheme,
There's relief beyond the rainbow in the blue;
We must summon up our courage;
We must dare again to dream,
And Tomorrow's finest promise can come true.

While our problems may be many,
And our spirits vexed may be,
Let the bolster of our faith submerge our fears;
With the good that life provides us
Our reward will surely be
That we never let it be a vale of tears.

To Philip

(On Receiving a Big Disappointment)

Another place, another time,
Your victory will brightly burn;
Your soul will soar, and you will find
The goal for which your young heart yearns.

Not all is lost; somebody cares—
Let courage rise 'mid strength and love;
And raise your shield, unsheathe your sword,
And let your challenge ring above.

Let not defeat becloud your view
Nor failure cast its bitter pall;
For, hark! Adventure waits anew
For you to answer to her call.

Who knows what triumph lies ahead
For you to taste its joys sublime—
A spring from which your soul is fed—
Another place, another time.

So That I Might

So that I might of earthly pleasures sip,
I drew my thoughts from worlds to me alone
Revealed; and with a smile on heart and lip,
That which by only carefree youth is known,
I flung my somber broodings to the winds
To toss and air and carry where they might,
And with a crowd of youthful, mirthful friends,
Betook myself to spend a gala night.

My friends a party joined with laughter loud;
Their feet kept rhythm with the music bold;
But I stood on the fringes of the crowd
And felt so very small and lone and cold.

Attempts at gaiety have come to naught;
Content am I to sit alone with thought.

Family Reunion

While some come from nearby, some come from afar;
While some come by airplane, still others by car.
They all gather in for their big annual fling,
And what hearty appetites do they all bring!

They eat while they're talking; they talk while they
     eat—
The barbeque, pasta; the salads, the sweets;
They swig down the sodas, the coolers, the beer;
And all the while great plans are laid for next year.

The while they play catch-up, all day tongues will wag;
The kids swim and tussle while grandmothers brag.
They match jobs and children and sport their new cars,
Comparing the engines and kicking the tires.

At last dusk announces the close of the day;
With kissing and hugging they go on their way;
With unashamed weeping for neighbors to see,
For love is abundant in this family.

Mother Mary, Walk with Me

Mary, maid of Nazareth,
Simple, pure, and fair of face;
Maid with sacred virtues blest,
Hail to thee, most full of grace!
As you walked in Galilee,
Mother Mary, walk with me.

With your mantle shaded blue,
Shield me from my foolish fears;
Give me courage, fresh and new;
Dry my silent, burning tears.
As you walked in Galilee,
Mother Mary, walk with me.

Mother of the Universe,
Help me in my direst need!
Shower me with boundless love;
Be my Mother, too, I plead!
As you walked in Galilee,
Mother Mary, walk with me.

Mary, maid of Nazareth,
Sweet and gentle—undefiled,
Through your intercession, guide,
Love, and keep this little child.
As you walked in Galilee,
Mother Mary, walk with me.

Not Mine to Keep

Not mine to keep—this baby's smile
With single tear in transient mood;
Mine just to have a little while
Till Youth shall steal his babyhood.

Not mine to keep—this breathless noon
With sunlit grass and dappled shade,
With baby birds in tuneless tune
And other wonders God has made.

Not mine to keep—this dear one's face
Replete with love in every line,
For marching time must keep its pace;
It cannot be forever mine.

Not mine to keep—true friendship's hand—
The golden bond companions give;
I must relinquish on command—
It only in my memory lives.

I cannot keep this little home;
It profits not to Fate revile;
For 'tis my destiny to roam,
Yet love I must—a little while.

The Funeral

Her form lay pale and still and cold
  Within the satin bed;
Her hands were folded as in prayer,
  A pillow 'neath her head.

It is a time to show reserve
  And take the proffered hand,
Accepting words of sympathy
  From those who understand.

And now the bells will sound their knell,
  And gentle words be said;
With prayer and song her form is laid
  In its eternal bed.

Then with the mourners gone away,
  Their own pathways to keep,
There's time enough to feel the pain—
  And time enough to weep.

On Saying "No"

It isn't very difficult
   To give the answer "No"—
The tongue cleaves in an "N" sound;
   The lips form into "O."

Suppose she's only two or three,
   With pony tail and bow;
Her pout is pretty as can be—
   You give the answer, "No."

Suppose the young teen begs and pleads
   To go where all kids go,
Perhaps to sample this or that—
   A firm, decisive "No!"

Suppose his eyes are soft and dark;
   He says he loves you so;
His arms are very strong and warm—
   The answer still is "No."

We learn as lifetime passes on,
   We reap the deeds we sow,
And character is being formed
   By listening to "No."

Bethlehem Babe

Refrain

Gloria! Gloria!
Jesus Christ is born!
Rejoice! Rejoice!
O happy Christmas morn!

A dark countryside,
An angelic host,
Good shepherds attending their sheep;
A bright, guiding star,
Wise men from afar,
A baby's soft slumber to keep
A still, little town that gave rest to a King;
A mother so lovely and mild;
The angels that to the dear Infant did sing;
A manger that cradled a Child.

Refrain

O wee bit of Life,
O great Gift from Heav'n,
O small hands that great empires sway;
O sweet, sleepy eyes
That must close before even;
O pure heart much fairer than day;
To You and You only this praise do we bring
From corners so far of the earth;
Till all this sphere and the Heavens above
Shall kneel as they knelt at Your birth.

Refrain

To My Child

For every tear you shed, my child,
  I shed one in my heart;
For every hurt that brings you pain,
  I feel the sting and smart.

I revel in each small success
  And sigh with every loss;
Your rainbows make my soul rejoice;
  Your burdens are my cross.

And if your way is dark and long,
  My path is twisted, too;
But if your spirit lifts in song,
  My glad heart sings with you.

Perhaps someday you'll have a child,
  And then you, too, will know
The feelings that engulf my heart
  And why I love you so!

Summer Vacation

My memory brings before my eyes
  Sweet scenes I never shall forget;
I see a night of star-swept skies—
  The blissful night when first we met.

I see us strolling hand-in-hand
  Beside the undulating sea,
Which, reaching from the golden sand,
  Embraces all infinity.

The sunny days beside the tide;
  The sailboat rides across the bay;
The hikes across the countryside—
  The many times we lost our way.

The picnic lunch beneath the trees;
  The magic of a mellow moon—
Yes, all are now mere memories
  Of bygone days that passed too soon.

Now summer's gone and so we tread
  Our individual paths again;
But what a lot we left unsaid—
  And, oh, to think what might have been.

Subway Bum

He's only a bum in the subway
With no home to lay down his head;
His clothes are his only possessions,
And newspapers make up his bed.

His waste fouls the dank subway stairwell,
And lice have infested his hair;
The crowds pass in faceless confusion,
Pretending he's not even there.

A handout will buy him some coffee,
Some soup, or a bottle of rum;
And the clock marks another day passing
In the life of a poor subway bum.

He's only a bum in the subway,
Living down 'neath the cold city streets;
But some mother bore him and loved him,
And some mother rocked him to sleep.

Entreaty

Oh, grant me that when I shall die,
  You will not bury me
In graveyard where cold bodies lie
  'Neath crosses orderly.
There names of humble are proclaimed
  And marble soars on high
To mark the honored graves of famed;
  But to the passers-by
  A name is but a name.

But, rather, lay me in the shade
  Of some tall, sheltering tree
Where sunlight in the leaves will play
  And frolic over me.
Erect no tombstone at my head—
  No slab to mark the spot;
Let grass and flowers grow instead
  And cover up the plot
  Of this, my final bed.

Ah, better 'tis to lie alone
  With but a humble mound
Where tangled briars around will roam
  And flowers dot the ground;
So when on earth I cease to plod,
  And dust to dust returns,
I'll lie alone beneath the sod;
  For this my spirit yearns—
  To rest with peace and God.

Where Are You Tonight?

Where are you tonight,
My little one, my precious one?
Where are you tonight,
Oh, my dear one?

I rocked you in your cradle
And sweetly held you near;
I watched you in your nursery
And dried your baby tears.

I saw you flourish daily
And grow in years and form;
You slipped the bonds of tending
And ventured into harm.

Into the world of passions,
Of drugs and neon bars,
Of knives and chains and pistols,
Of sleek and racy cars.

Will teachings hold you steady?
Is faith what it should be?
Will heartstrings bind you closely
And bring you back to me?

Where are you tonight,
My little one, my precious one?
Where are you tonight,
Oh, my dear one?

Let It Be

I thank You, Lord, for this new day—
  For this terrestrial morning;
For bud and tree, for earth and sea,
  And all things fair a-borning.

The bitter cup of yesterday
  Was difficult to swallow;
Let not my heart forever smart,
  Nor in regret to wallow.

Tomorrow offers naught but joy;
  Oh, let me taste her pleasure
That I may live to take and give
  Your love in fullest measure.

With every challenge squarely met—
  Each obstacle and care—
I'll see Your love shine forth above
  And know that You are there.

Oh, Cat

Oh, cat upon my windowsill,
Do you enjoy the sights you see—
The pretty birds with pointy bills,
The squirrels that leap from tree to tree?

Oh, cat asleep upon my bed,
Are you as cozy as you seem,
With nodding head and fluffy tail
Curled 'round you in a kitty dream?

Oh, little prisoner in my home,
Contained by love and not by bars,
You're safe from brutal elements,
And safe from varmints, safe from cars.

You knead my person without fear,
And nestle close to ever prove,
While purring pleasure in my ear,
The reaches of your kitty love.

The Child Grows Tall

He is this child of yours by birth or choice,
This you reborn, or else you've chosen free
To make the reaches of your heart rejoice
And mold him with your careful artistry—
This lump of living clay, this child so dear—
Into a being filled with strength and love,
And disciplined by all your standards clear
To stand up in Life's storms and always prove
That as the twig is bent, the child will grow;
And heavy is the burden that you bear
To see that he will surely gain and know
The qualities that will his way prepare—
Instilling sense of values while he's small,
For as the hour grows late, the child grows tall.

Go Down to Jerusalem

Go down, down, down to Jerusalem,
And there you will find your cross!

Is your brother tired and empty
    And hungering for food?
Take from your ample larder
    And you'll profit for the good.

Is your sister sick and lonely
    And weary of her lot?
A gentle hand; a loving word—
    You've much compassion brought.

Is your brother cold and trembling?
    You've coats enough for two;
So share them as the Master
    Would ever have you do.

Is your neighbor grieved about you
    With friendship at a loss?
Cast pride away; extend your hand;
    You'll never miss the cost.

Is the path before you dreary
    With troubles by the score?
Your load will be made lighter
    By the cross that Jesus bore.

Go down, down, down to Jerusalem,
And there you will find your cross!

One Little Candle

Within Life's valley, dark and drear,
The sun and moon refuse to shine;
And evil forces hover near
To threaten every righteous sign.

Yet in my humble state I find,
If I can cause a tiny gleam,
I'll light a candle for mankind,
Though it may shed a feeble beam.

Amid the dread and anxious gloom
And through confusion rife with fear,
Here I will let my candle bloom
While bringing consolation near.

Until my bell shall sound its knell,
And through the dark I need not grope,
Behold my shining sentinel—
'Tis this my candle, this my hope.

Shadows in My Heart

I do not hear the myriad birds
  Singing on bush and tree;
I do not see the bonny flowers
  Blooming o'er the lea.

I do not heed the flaming sun,
  Flooding the earth with light;
I do not see the glittering stars
  Piercing the Nubian night.

I do not hear my many friends
  Greeting me each day;
All my hopes and all my dreams
  Have turned a dreary gray.

I know but this—that once you were
  And that you now are not;
I know the grief and dark despair
  Of love not soon forgot.

Oh, how can I live remembering,
  And again in life take part?
Must I face life unwavering
  With shadows in my heart?

My Squirrel

You trespass gaily in my trees,
O you of dark and beady eye—
A furry streak of gray and white—
Then balance on your perch so high.

Your bushy tail must be your pride;
You swish it quickly left and right,
Expressing your anxiety,
Perhaps in wrath, perhaps in fright.

You venture freely on my stoop
And peer in boldly through my door
As if to ask for trick or treat—
You beggar! Where's your winter store?

I watch in wonder and delight
Your circus act across my trees;
My friendly squirrel, come be my guest—
Your antics always charm and please.

The Clown

His mood was always jolly,
  And he wore a friendly smile;
He was full of fun and folly,
  And humor was his style.

He cheered the little children
  With games of wit and skill;
They laughed to see him coming.
  For he gave them quite a thrill.

He kissed the older ladies
  And chucked their trembling chins;
His humor was contagious
  And always brought a grin.

But when the day was over,
  And night was drawing near,
He wept into his pillow—
  A clown's own secret tears.

Because the Night

Because the night precedes the dawn
With dark forebodings ever near,
God set the stars to twinkle on
And gave the friendly moon for cheer.

In mountains high or valleys low,
He lights our pathways with His beams;
And where the wild winds fiercely blow,
We still can find a guiding gleam.

We gird our souls to journey far
And venture forth whate'er the toll,
From silv'ry star to silv'ry star
With everlasting dawn our goal.

The Wall and the Bridge

You built a wall around your stone-cold heart,
Protecting it from casual passers-by,
Rejecting dreams disposed to fall apart,
Refusing loves that only made you cry.
You fenced my deep and ardent feelings out
And left me with my dampened hopes and pain,
Accepting vague suspicions, seeds of doubt,
Full rampant in your safe, secure domain.
I took the dare unbidden and unsought
And laid my tender passions at your feet,
While hoping that a miracle be wrought;
And by my supplications gentle, sweet,
I built a bridge across your mighty wall;
And now your heart rejoices in Love's call.

The Empty Swing

Gone now are the sounds of childish chatter;
Gone the rosy cheeks and dimpled knees;
Gone the cherished dreams that really matter—
The empty swing sways slowly in the breeze.

Now gone the fingerprints along the hallways;
Gone the earnest, childish tries to please;
Gone the laughter, gone for now and always—
The empty swing sways slowly in the breeze.

Gone the goodnight hugs and sticky kisses;
Gone each chance my hungry heart would seize
To spread the love my soul so sorely misses—
The empty swing sways slowly in the breeze.

I Need Not Die

I need not die to write of death,
  Nor yet exult to write of joy;
But search I must my length and breadth
  To all my writing skills employ.

A heart disposed to passions sweet—
  A soul imbued with love and care—
A mind-embracing reverie—
  A facile pen inclined to dare.

You must not take as personal
  All words upon my printed page;
While they are mine, perhaps they still
  Are products of my muse's rage.

While some evince my life and times,
  And all are off'rings of my pen,
Some might be fantasies sublime,
  Or just reflect what might have been.

Please Thank Me Not

Please thank me not for any gift
  I may on you bestow;
Already I have reaped my thanks—
  There is no more to owe.

I am forever gratified;
  In giving I have willed
That it is ever in the act
  I am myself fulfilled.

Day Person

The sun has vanished from the friendly skies,
While darkness has descended once again;
And nighttime with its thousand piercing eyes
Peers at me through my crystal window pane.
My warm and pleasant house becomes a place
Of dark forebodings only night can bring,
Like shadows crossing past the moon's scarred face
And causing all my courage to take wing.
The creaking board that wasn't there before
Forewarns of danger coming in the night;
The rattling of the wind about the door
Compounds anxieties, produces fright;
But morning always dawns both clear and bright,
And once more I have made it through the night.

Above the Storm

Oh, give me splendrous wings of white, dear God,
And let me learn to fly above the storm—
The lightning's flash, the thunder's roar, the flood—
Oh, grant a fearless journey safe from harm.

Please free me from the dark and troubled dreams
That make me fretfully cry out aloud,
And let me travel unimpeded, free,
My feet, perhaps, to skim the fleecy clouds.

While soaring high above the teeming strife,
I'll wing in peace and equanimity
And render thanks for everlasting life—
Someday to rest where all my treasures be.

For then I'll lay my heavy burdens down,
And problems of this world will be transformed;
But till I claim with joy my promised crown,
Oh, Father, let me fly above the storm.

My Angel

I have an angel guardian
  Who watches over me;
He tends me with a quiet grace
  I neither hear nor see.

He sets my path on safest ways,
  And guides my stumbling feet
Lest I should venture far astray
  Upon Life's mountains steep.

I feel his warnings in the night
  And heed his silent call;
My path is followed without fright
  Beneath his shadow tall.

Is he remiss if I should dash
  My foot against a stone?
Not so; 'tis Satan lurking near
  To claim me for his own.

So down the long and twisted road
  I travel without fear
Because I feel his guiding touch
  And know my angel's near.

You Made Your Choice

You made your choice, my wishes notwithstanding;
Your life is yours to live the way you choose;
And now we both must live with your decision—
So great the penalty if you should lose.

I did not lift one finger to dissuade you,
Although my heart was full of unshed tears;
And now I grieve and live with silent sorrow;
You made your choice, my dear, my dear, my dear!

We will not know until the Great Hereafter
Which path was true and which one missed the way;
So till we reach that place of joy and laughter,
I'll watch and wait and hope and love and pray.

The Song of the Wind

All nations quail before my frightful power;
I scatter bleak destruction o'er the land;
I cause the angry clouds to seethe and glower;
And mighty oceans move at my command.

When nighttime's gloom begins to mass and thicken,
Outside your walls you hear my eerie wails;
You hesitate and feel your pulses quicken
And think of crying souls and ghostly tales.

I set the tops of stately trees in motion;
They pirouette and bow before my face.
I snatch men's hats upon a playful notion
And bid their owners join a comic race.

I sometimes show a nature mild and gentle
And move sleek sailboats in a placid cove;
I ruffle little petticoats, and, if choosing,
I can bend and kiss the petal of a rose.

The Breakup of a Non-Marriage

We skipped the records in the township hall,
The gown, the flowers, the church, and folderol;
We made our commitment, one to the other,
Without ceremonies
  Or trite and phony phrases.

The days sped by, or was it years?
And everything fell into its proper place;
We knew the bliss of loving and of being loved,
And the knowledge.
  Of peacefulness and of caring.

It was just the two of us, aloof from all conventions,
Living our lives for, yet independent of each other,
With the world sometimes with and sometimes apart
From the earnest lifetime
  That we were carving together.

And then, incredibly, the fragile magic vanished,
And there was nothing to sustain our frail resolves.
Easy, you say, to call it quits with no entanglements;
You merely go your separate ways,
  And that is that.

Why, then, do I feel both bereaved and abandoned,
Bereft of happiness and hopeless of the future,
Sitting and sifting the dead, dusty ashes
Of my ruined dreams, and wondering what happened,
  And how and where and why?

On Diapers

We one time bought them made of cloth,
Of gauze, perhaps, in bird's-eye style;
For winter they were flannelette
With soft and fuzzy, cozy pile.

We washed them with the purest soap
And hung them on the line to dry;
They blew like small sails in the breeze
Beneath a bright and azure sky.

We folded them with tender care
And smoothed till each was wrinkle-free;
They bore the scent of outdoor air,
As fresh and fragrant as could be.

We buy them now to throw away,
All sized to fit each small behind—
A style for her; a style for him—
With sticky tapes of finest kind.

We must move forward with the times,
And new advancements are quite fine;
But, oh, the sweet nostalgic sight
Of diapers blowing on the line.

Surrender

How many times I've passed this way—
 I'm weary of the view.
I've seen the light of myriad days;
 There's nothing for me new.

I've climbed a thousand mountains,
 And I've known the depths beneath;
I've borne a thousand burdens,
 And I've known a thousand griefs.

Life's crown has lost its luster,
 And the years have claimed their toll;
I'm tired of new beginnings,
 And I want to rest my soul.

Forgive me this surrender, Lord;
 I've given up my quest.
Do not withhold my last reward;
 I only want to rest.

Grandma

She was a country woman
  With simple, rustic ways;
Without sophistication,
  She spent her earthly days.

Her face had lost its beauty;
  Her form was frail and thin;
Her nose was slightly Roman
  And angled toward her chin.

Her cotton dress was faded
  And not the latest style;
Although her trials were many,
  She braved them with a smile.

At home she bore her children
  And nurtured them with care;
Her love was not flamboyant,
  But always it was there.

Her table was provided
  From her little garden's store—
Though plain and very simple,
  There was never need for more.

While history won't extol her
  As the years so quickly fade,
Still we shall long remember
  The difference she made.

Glory Road

When we choose Christ as our Savior,
There's a price that we must pay,
For the road to Glory's paved with many tears;
We must bear our burden gladly
And must never be afraid;
There's no place on Glory Road for futile fears.

Glory Road is dim and narrow
And has snares at every bend,
And the headaches and the heartaches claim their toll;
But the good and faithful traveler
Has the Savior as a Friend,
And He lifts and buoys the tired and flagging soul.

When the tempest blows around us,
Or the bright sun burns our skin,
And the splinters from the cross may cause us pain,
We must seek a silver lining,
And we'll triumph in the end—
There's no end to walk the Glory Road again.

When eternal dawn has broken,
And the fog has slipped away,
There will lie in shining splendor our abode;
And a crown of stars we'll merit
For our faith along the way,
Free to all who choose to walk the Glory Road.

The Empty Nest

First, there were four of us, making a home;
We were a happy and gay family;
Together we laughed as we played and we loved—
Teddy Bear, Baby and Daddy and Me.

Teddy grew tattered and ragged and old;
His coat was as frazzled and worn as could be;
We sadly consigned him to his last reward,
Leaving just Baby and Daddy and Me.

Baby grew taller and wedded a bride;
No lassie was ever as lonely as she;
They formed a new union distinctly apart
And left quite alone only Daddy and Me.

Life has grown simpler, but, oh, what a void
That yearns for the glad times of sweet memory
When there were together the four of the past—
Teddy Bear, Baby and Daddy and Me.

There's Christy

There's Christy on the sofa,
  And Christy on the chair;
There's Christy on the carpet—
  There's Christy everywhere.

There's Christy down the hallway,
  And Christy on the stair;
There's Christy on the dresser—
  At least, there's Christy's hair.

Of course, we'll still adore her
  While overlooking that
We've problems in attending
  A shedding, long-haired cat.

Courage

You say defeat and sense of loss confound you,
The while there's darkest gloom on every side;
And you've despaired of any new tomorrows,
And now your aching heart broke down and cried?

Command the strength to venture ever onward;
Futility must not lay siege to you;
You must endure the raging storm about you
Until a brilliant rainbow you will view.

Hold fast, hang on; there'll be a brighter dawning
With promise of a far more kindly fate;
In order to receive this precious bounty,
You must consent to persevere and wait.

Supportive Time will heal your shattered feelings;
And shortly Life will better, brighter seem—
Arising from the ashes of your passions
Shall be another hope, another dream.

A Simple Plea

Dear Lord, give me the strength to be
The things Your love has taught to me.
Make me more loving in my heart,
In others' trials to do my part.
Guide my stumbling, wayward feet
Over the trail so rough and steep;
Clutch my hand and draw me back
If I try to leave your chosen track.
Let me not love sin nor strife—
Give me a broader view of life.
Remove all smugness from my soul;
Let not old sorrows take their toll
To make me shallow, bitter, sad
Because of joys I might have had.
Teach me to enjoy Life's beauty
And to my neighbor do my duty.
Assure me of the infinitesimal price
Of each whole-hearted sacrifice.
May I give all that I can give
To make earth a finer place to live,
That when I depart for Higher Ground,
I'll leave it better than it was found.
Thank You for life, for health, for food,
For love, happiness, and all that's good;
And, God, as you look down on me,
Lift up this prayer—a simple plea.

Home

While I may wander far and wide,
  From sea to flashing sea,
There's nothing quite like coming home
  To where my heart shall be.

The grandeur of the mountain peaks,
  The canyons far below
Impress and thrill, but always still,
  It's home I want to go.

The seashore leaves a lasting mark;
  The city's treats amuse;
Still, in the final preference,
  It's home I'll always choose

The little house is old and plain
  But peaceful as can be;
And faded shingles can't abate
  The joy it holds for me.

So, though I travel up and down,
  And far away I roam,
It's good to know within my breast
  I'll soon be going home.

My Silent Prayer

Did you hear my prayer, dear Father—
  The prayer I prayed today—
The wordless supplication
  My heart sent up Your way?

Though laden with my heavy cares,
  I tried to go to sleep;
But sheer despair and gripping fears
  Through consciousness did creep.

The while my lips were silent
And thoughts were vacant, too,
My heart still breathed an earnest prayer
That lifted up to You.

Did you hear my prayer, dear Father—
The prayer I prayed today—
The wordless supplication
My heart sent up your way?

The Fan

The fan on the ceiling goes 'round and around,
Its blades whirling blurry and dim;
And over the warm air they swiftly do skim,
  As the fan on the ceiling goes 'round.

The doors of my lifetime go 'round and around;
I'm frequently back where I've been,
But throughout each new day I stoutly will fend,
  As the fan on the ceiling goes 'round.

Metamorphosis

Old Winter donned his long, white robe
And strutted boldly through the town;
The scant leaves on the pin oak trees
Gave forth a rustling, whispering sound.

While ice and snow in harsh array
Preclude the faintest hope of spring,
The frigid winds tear at the trees
And hurl their frosty bite and sting.

But ice one day will melt away,
And winds cannot forever blow;
For, lo, with time a crocus blooms
And lifts its head above the snow.

The earth's rebirth revives our hopes
And sends our spirits soaring high;
Once more we feel the breath of spring
And gaze into a soft blue sky.

Send Rain Again

For the farmer and his fields,
For crops to reach their highest yield,
For the fruit and for the grain,
    Send rain, O God,
    Send rain again!

For the gardens, large and small,
For flowers, grass, and trees so tall;
Do not all our prayers disdain;
    Send rain, O God,
    Send rain again!

For our feathered friends so dear,
For our waters cold and clear
For creatures of the woods and plain,
    Send rain, O God,
    Send rain again!

Grant this arid land relief;
Deliver us from drought and grief;
Have mercy on Your parched domain;
    Send rain, O God,
    Send rain again!

Hear the rain dove's mournful note,
Adding prayers to our refrain
With plaintive pleadings from his throat;
    Send rain, O God,
    Send rain again!

The River

My life is a boat on a River;
With Faith, Hope, and Love as my crew,
I muster my skills for the journey
And sail forth with confidence new.

At times there is peace on the River;
And calmly, serenely I row,
My crew ever faithful beside me
As through the still waters I go.

Sometimes the clouds thicken in anger,
And crashes of thunder I hear;
My boat pitches wildly in tumult
And leaves my heart quaking with fear.

I cry to the God of the River,
Beseeching with fright and alarm;
He stretches His hand o'er my vessel
And saves it from danger and harm.

And when my life's journey is ended,
With sails blowing brightly and free,
I'll guide surely down to the Harbor,
And there safe at anchor I'll be.

While Strolling One Day

While strolling one day through a meadow,
  Not thinking—just dreaming along,
My mind overflowed with contentment,
  And deep in my heart was a song.

The morning was bursting with splendor;
  The sun, rising blazing and bold,
Which, with the flame Nature did lend her,
  Was gilding the meadow with gold.

The grass, bending under my footsteps,
  Was wet from an early spring shower;
And in its recesses was hiding
  A treasure of Nature—a flower.

It stood, a young queen of the valley,
  Enthroned in a palace of grass,
Accepting, as token of homage,
  A kiss from the breeze as it passed.

I knelt by its side in the meadow;
  And there 'neath the bright azure skies,
I gazed in the depths of a flower—
  Saw beauty on earth summarized.

Judgment Day

That day to each of us shall surely come
When we'll be judged upon our rights and wrongs,
As we shall seek our fair, celestial home
And gather with the blest about the throne.
There I shall never brag of charity,
Nor vouch for right in everything I've done;
I shall not freely flaunt for all to see
My strength in every earthly battle won.
I shall not proffer every word as truth,
Nor swear the finest doctrine I partook;
But as I stand to humbly plead for ruth,
Then I shall open wide Life's telling book
And cry from glorious body undefiled,
"Oh, God, my gracious Lord, behold Thy child!"

The Front Porch

A front porch is a friendly place
With happy times recorded there—
The loved ones and the family friends,
The dog, the cat, the rocking chair.

The porch swing where young lovers sat
Beneath a full and radiant moon
Brings back a flood of memories
Of mellow days with hearts in tune.

The ivy through the trellis twines
With sunlight dappled into lace,
And cozy thoughts pervade the scene—
A front porch is a friendly place.

In all our sunset years we'll sit
And reminisce without a care
The while we savor things we love—
The dog, the cat, the rocking chair.

When I in Deepest Melancholy

When I in deepest melancholy sink;
When all my good intentions miss their mark;
When life grows grayer, duller; when to think
Means only that depression grows more dark;
When battle after battle must be fought,
And nothing looms before me but defeat;
When all objectives that my soul has sought
Still far outstrip me with their wings so fleet;
Then do I grimly doubt the worth of life;
Then do I dimly view success's throne
That lures me on to senseless, futile strife;
Then am I, though in sad and different tone,
Inclined to join with gay Mehitabel
In voicing, "Whatthehell, oh, whatthehell."

On Work

St. Joseph labored with his hands
While making articles of wood;
He knew what all mankind should know—
That work is noble; work is good.

There is no prize for indolence;
Nor is there praise for laziness;
The one who shirks should feel the ache
Of deep and profound emptiness.

As honest work makes honest men
And gives us reason to arise,
To be worthwhile has its reward
In grace before our Master's eyes.

This remedy for idle hands
Gives living proof of human worth;
So may we wisely use the time
Allotted us on God's good earth.

Our work should highly valued be,
Exalted till our labor's done;
So let us teach our children well,
As Joseph taught his Holy Son.

Accomplishment

Beneath my flying fingers deft,
With hook and yarn I weave a form
In patterned lace with colors true—
A shawl I weave, so soft and warm;
    And those who look upon it will
    Behold the product of my skill.

Within my ever-gentle arms,
A child is guided in his youth,
And loved and taught with tender care
The way of God and Light and Truth,
    That He who watches from above
    Beholds the product of my love.

In precious moments day by day,
The fabric of my life I weave;
My thoughts and actions form the web
Of what my efforts will achieve;
    And those who light me to my goal
    Behold the product of my soul.

Resolve

When presented with a problem,
Don't attempt to run away;
It will lurk around a corner
And return another day.

'Tis much better far to seize it
And confront it face-to-face;
It may cower in confusion
And retreat without a trace.

When you bring to bear your logic,
And your courage comes to fore,
You'll reduce the foe to ashes
And your confidence will soar.

Whether compromise or triumph,
Satisfaction will be found;
And you'll feel contentment knowing
That today you stood your ground.

Nine and Eight and Four

Their hair hangs soft in silken strands;
Their angel smiles I fast adore;
Their clear, young eyes are full of trust,
For they are nine and eight and four.

Their fresh, young minds are open wide
For bright, new vistas to explore;
A grand, wide world is beckoning,
For they are nine and eight and four.

I strive to teach what they should learn,
Lest Time escape forevermore;
For character is being built
While they are nine and eight and four.

Today I'll shower them with love,
As this brief span shall be no more,
And hold them dearly in my arms
While they are nine and eight and four.

Maytime

Ching-a-ling, ching-a-ling,
Come and make merry-o,
Lift up your voices and joyously sing;
Ching-a-ling, ching-a-ling,
Come and be cheery-o
Winter lies vanquished, and now it is spring.

Ring-a-ling, ding-a-ling,
Ring in the zephyr breeze,
Kissing the mountain, the valley and stream;
Buds are a-blossoming;
June is o'possuming;
Pregnant with roses, she smiles in her dream.

Ching-a-ling, ching-a-ling,
Ring in the spring delights;
Banish the dark, dismal winter so gray;
Cast care and worry out;
Join in the gala shouts;
Earth is rejoicing; all hail to the May!

Remembrance

I'm here on earth for but a little while
And, passing through, may never long impress;
But let me give each friend a cheerful smile
And try my human failings to redress.

In someone's soul in my memory will live
In ways by which I've touched another's heart
If I will offer all that I can give
And to each day my faith and truth impart.

If all my efforts light a tiny spark,
Then let the record show how hard I tried
To leave some print, some signature, some mark,
And in this granted wish be gratified.

Death Enters

I gazed down on the face so pale;
I stroked the thinning, silvered hair.
The aged form was spare and frail,
Which in its prime had been so fair.

I held the still hand in my own,
And knelt and said a silent prayer;
Then swiftly rose and left the room—
I felt another Presence there.

That's Good Enough for Me

The floor is worn;
The curtain's drab
And faded as can be;
The couch has seen much better days—
That's good enough for me!

The wall clock ticks
When it should tock;
Its chime is half off-key;
The mirror's silver needs repair—
That's good enough for me!

The table knives
Don't match the forks
Like high society;
The porcelain has lost its glaze—
That's good enough for me!

The caring word,
The tender touch,
The love that all can see;
The happiness that fills my home—
That's good enough for me!

Journey

I thank you, God, each day for life,
  For temporal bliss and love,
For strength to stand amid the strife,
  With grace from Heav'n above.

I thank You for each tree and flower—
  All earthly beauty fair;
I thank you for my heavenly goal
  And faith to take me there.

I do not ask my lot be free
  From trouble and from care;
But let my earthly burden be
  No more than I can bear.

And may my voice in vibrant song
  Before Your throne arise,
When I behold my happy home
  Eternal in the skies.

The World Is Likened

The world is likened to a garden fair
With flowers, trees, and fauna growing there;
And through it runs a river we call Life,
Upon whose surface bubbles rage and strive
And symbolize distraught humanity,
Which struggles, racing onward to the sea
Of great accomplishment and worthy gain.
The foamy surface, churned by frequent rain,
Collects more bubbles, which, in turn, the fray
Do join and battle for supremacy;
But 'neath the babble, swift and cold and gray,
The river surges on relentlessly.
Then do you think, if worst should come to worst,
The stream would note if one small bubble burst?

My Garden

Some gardens are for outdoor fun,
While others grow to fill a need;
No matter what the reason be—
You must have faith to plant a seed.

There must pour forth the gentle rain;
There must shine down the kindly sun;
My faithful work may go for naught
If Nature's teamwork is not won.

I long to see the stems of green,
All staked like Nature's sentinels,
And touch each bush, each leaf, each sprig
That ventures forth from tiny cells.

Dear God, I've sorely yearned for spring;
I've languished long with ice and snow;
Now look with favor on my toil
And help my little garden grow!

Every Day's Child

Each Monday's full of promise;
Each Tuesday's bright and fair,
While Wednesday's made for doing;
And Thursday's time to care.
With each new week before you,
Take joy in every day,
And never live for Friday
To wish your life away!

Guideposts

I tread Life's rough and rugged ground
And find that guideposts clear abound,
For many footprints I have found.
In valleys deep I find a light,
On mountains high a signal bright;
In woodlands dark, without affright,
I journey bold and dauntlessly
To where eternal treasures be
Beyond the shining, placid sea.

With vision clear, I find my way
As clouds lift on eternal day,
And footprints ever guide my way.

Amid the scattered guideposts rife,
A message clear above the strife
Comes echoing along my life.

So I shall bravely carry on
Till shadows break as night is done
To find the Everlasting Sun.

His Brokenness

I cannot heal the halt and lame,
  Nor give sight to the blind;
But I can take my brother's hand
  And touch his heart and mind.

I cannot cause perpetual joy
  To flood my brother's way;
But I can offer kindliness
  To light a dreary day.

I may not still the gripping fears
  That to his lot may fall;
But I can guide my brother's heart
  To heed the Master's call.

I cannot give complete relief
  From sorrow and from pain;
But I can lift him from his grief
  And help him strive again.

My life must be a beacon bright
  With saving graces blest
That pierces through the fearful night
  And heals his brokenness.

On Riches

If it should happen that one day
  I should acquire great riches,
I would not cast it all away
  To satisfy my wishes.

I would not hoard it in a cave—
  My lovely, fabulous treasure;
Nor hide it in secluded spots
  To count it at my leisure.

Nor would I give it to the poor
  To aid them in their trouble;
Nor would I put it in a bank
  To try to make it double.

I would not give it to my foes
  To try to win them over;
Nor give a morsel to my friends
  Although I be in clover.

And none would go to aid the sick
  Nor to the lame be given;
I would not give it to the Church
  To help lost souls to Heaven.

But if this wealth should come to me,
  The thing to do, it seems,
Is try my very level best
  Not to disturb the dream.

Shakespeare

When every bird in England built its nest,
The earth with mirth and melody was filled,
As young and old with writing powers blest
With flowing pen each trade and art did gild.

And then there entered on Life's changing stage
An actor with a writing gift sublime,
Who was acclaimed the favorite of his Age,
Whose fame would linger far beyond his time.

Ranked high above the writers of his day,
He plied with zest and zeal his faithful pen;
He viewed this temporal life as but a play—
The people as but characters therein.

He played his role both graciously and well
Until at last the curtain on him fell.

Peace Be with You

Of earthly gifts mankind is given,
None exceeds the gift of peace;
Relayed from brother unto brother,
It magnifies with each release.

Our hunger can be borne in silence;
Even pain can be endured;
But when the sore heart writhes in turmoil,
True peace can never be assured.

While peace is free to all who seek it,
The heart must calm and open be
With readiness to take and offer
To all who are God's family.

A sense of peace can come through caring,
From doing what we know is good,
From opening our hearts and sharing,
Be it love or time or food.

So flee not into distant mountains,
There to hide your woe and care;
For flowing from abundant fountains
Is peace to keep and peace to share.

Grandma's Cookies

At Grandma's house on holidays,
  Up to her arms in dough,
She used to bake some cookies that
  Set our tastebuds aglow.

We always smelled their fragrance sweet
  When we came in the door;
It rose in clouds of lusciousness
  Up to the second floor.

The nutmeg, cloves, and cinnamon
  Combined to make a treat;
With chocolate chips and fresh pecans—
  A culinary feat!

Oh, you may have the apple pie;
  Likewise the chocolate cake;
Just leave for me the cookies like
  My grandma used to bake.

Building Blocks

He is so precious in your eyes—
This little one you hold today;
In him you place your highest hopes
And lovingly prepare his way.

As block by block his talents grow,
His future progress knows no bars;
For while he builds his little blocks,
He builds a future steered by stars.

And as the years speed swiftly by,
He'll grow mature in form and face;
And, if God willing, he'll receive
Abundances of hope and grace.

His strength must bear the stress of Life
With courage firm and faith supreme,
To build his castle to the skies,
Be it of brick or steel or dreams.

There Is a Season

An eastern glow,
A morning star,
The breaking of the day;
A breeze that blows
The heavens ajar;
The sun's first gentle ray.

It's time for work
Or love or hate;
To die or bring to birth;
To sail the seas,
Or skim the clouds,
Or till the fertile earth.

It's time to teach,
And time to learn
And time for joy or sorrow;
It's time to strive,
Or time to wish
And dream about tomorrow.

It's time for might
And time for fun,
And time for self-denial;
It's time to fight
And time to run,
Or time to face Life's trial.

No time for fears;
No time to fret;
No time to spend in sighing.
No time for tears
Or sore regret;
The day will soon be dying.

An evening hush,
A twilight sigh,
Too faint for man to hear;
A western blush,
A day that dies,
And God seems very near.

Did I Offend?

Did I offend with word too sharply spoken—
An errant word too hasty to recall?
Did I distress you with a promise broken,
Incurring your displeasure from it all?

Abjectly humble am I now approaching
To beg forgiveness on my bended knee,
And swear that there will never be encroaching;
I'll neither rude nor basely callous be.

I'll spread my lifetime's earnest hopes before you
And weave around you webs of splendid dreams;
I'll vow by all that's sacred I adore you
And prove love can be trustful as it seems.

For I would place you on a pedestal
From which, in my rapt view, you'd never fall.

Fleeting Sunshine

There's sunshine in my soul today;
   There's music in my heart;
There's a happy glow along the way
   That shines where shadows part.

There's music from an unseen choir
   That brightens every thought;
Enchantment waits within each hour,
   And love with beauty wrought.

There's friendship valued more than gold;
   There's happiness supreme;
There's laughter, youth, and joy untold
   That shimmers like a dream.

But shadows lurk along the way
   Till when this bliss has passed;
Though sunshine's in my soul today,
   There's chance it will not last.

Black Magic

At night when others are asleep
  And peacefully are dreaming,
I softly to my window creep,
  Where moonlight pale is beaming.

Into the vault of blackest ink
  I gaze with admiration,
And deep within my mind I think
  Of wonders of creation.

And when my heart with pain is fraught,
  Which callous friends have given,
I seek where mortals all have sought
  And turn my eyes to Heaven.

No matter if I am distressed,
  Forlorn or dismal feeling,
I'm conscious of a sense of rest
  And calmness o'er me stealing.

The beauty of the pensive night
  Is so inspiration-giving,
I feel that Life—wrong or right—
  Is really worth the living.

As silvery points high in the night
  Are glittering from afar,
My soul is calm; my heart is light
  For having touched a star.

On Losing Weight

Of Life's most cruel surprises,
  There's nothing I have found
Like stepping on the scale to see
  I've gained another pound.

Though calories are almost nil
  (I'm starving day by day),
My errant scale with hateful spite
  Still goes the other way.

I'll bash the fiend to rubble
  So from its yoke I'm free,
And buy a magic mirror;
  Then slim and lovely be.

Retrospect

So many things once, long ago,
  Loomed large in my young view;
So many problems, joys, and woes,
  Hopes, dreams, and trials, too;
But slowly all their worth and charm
  Diminished through the years;
Things which seem very foolish now
  At one time wrang heart's tears.
But they grew from a childish soul,
  Quite free from stain within;
And, knowing this, I must respect
  The things so vital then.

Oh, Time, Stand Still

Oh, Time, stand still and cease your frenzied turning;
My life at last has found my dreams fulfilled;
And there remains no searching, burning yearning;
My prayers are answered and my castles built.

When I behold the world in all its splendor,
My soul's hard-pressed to register it all;
The bright reflections of my Eden's grandeur
Consume my senses and my heart enthrall.

I feel my loves so sacred and so tender
Surround my heart with never-ending joy;
And now my soul, in ecstasy remembered
Proclaims my faith, my soaring spirits buoys.

The golden circle of my friends surrounds me,
Steadfast and true throughout the fleeing years;
No whisper of a lack of faith confounds me,
Full free of doubts; full free of latent fears.

With no more need to strive for hope to leaven,
I reconcile my soul with sweet release;
Oh, Time, stand still, and let this be my Heaven
With joyful heart and tranquil mind at peace.

The Death of an Aspen

It stood for fifty years or more,
  Its branches reaching for the sky;
It weathered sun and rain and storm
  And kept its head up proud and high.

The gentle breezes in its boughs
  Inspired its leaves to spin and turn
From green to white in fairy dance—
  A sight that caused the soul to burn.

But Mother Nature stretched her hand
  And willed the boughs to blanch and die;
Devoid of twinkling leaves, they etched
  Like skeletons against the sky.

The woodsman's blade no mercy showed
  As deep within the flesh it ground;
And, limb by limb, with stunning force
  It, sorely stricken, thundered down.

No more will squirrels a haven find,
  Nor twittering songsters greet the dawn;
No more will branches weave and sway
  And cast their shadows on the lawn.

A naked stump alone remains,
  Exposed for all the world to see;
But my mind's eye still fast recalls
  The dancing of the aspen tree.

Fireflies

At dusk they light the sunset sky
  With glowing points both near and far;
While some will rise and flee away,
  Still some I'll capture in my jar.

I chase and catch with gentle care
  And cradle them with sheer delight
Until within the jar they slip
  To be my prisoners for the night.

They give my soul a happy glow—
  These little messengers of light,
Who with their talents glint and gleam
  And brighten up a summer night.

Along your way, take heed of this:
  No matter how distressed you are,
You, too, can brave the dismal night
  And carry fireflies in a jar.

My Final Call

When I receive my last, my final call,
Will I be ready and prepared to go?
Or will there be some duty, large or small,
I'll leave unfinished in my work below—
Some cause unchampioned or some prize unclaimed;
And was my duty foisted off instead
When burden bested this, my human frame;
Oh, better far than leave a prayer unsaid.
Or was some vote uncast, some plans mislaid;
And were intentions left in disarray?
Such trifles will in mem'ry swiftly fade
In larger scene of recollection's sway.

But never, sure as there's a Heaven above,
May it be said that I neglected love.

Index